Legacy Bound and Memory Burdened

Charlene Nagy

Presentation by *BookLeaf Publishing*

Web: www.bookleafpub.com

E-mail: info@bookleafpub.com

ISBN: 978-93-95890-15-1

First edition 2022

For you Dad.

Home

Daylight's final breath of golden glow
Resisting the growing reach of violet shadow
Cloaking the verdure in it's cool embrace
The scent of mist gathering in the dusk strewn
pines

Whispering leaves in the eve's gentle breeze
I yearn to walk along the starlit path with you
once more
To watch the silvery moon cast it's magic over
the mirrored heavens
Transforming inky vastness into shimmering
stardust

The perfume of memories long gone

Awakens my mind and brings me home

Spring

Frozen fear thawing
In the sunlit warmth of hope
Strong will unfurling

Trillium

Soft white petals
So clean and pure

Peaking through the crusted snow
Reaching toward spring's gossamer light

As the air begins to warm
Spirits high with anticipation

The promise of new beginnings
The first blush of hope reclaimed

Promise

Earth charred and barren
Blackened carnage lining the course
Soot and ash lingering testimony
Of flame and smoke's remorse

Desolation laid bare
Existence come to it's end
New growth straining upward
Life begins to bloom again

Imbolc

5

Gathering grey, clouds the heavens
Sweetness of rain on the air
Silvery leaves turning upwards
Cool wind through fields bare

The downpour is cleansing
Droplets soaking my hair
Moss blanketed loam bedding
Mist dampened despair

Gossamer Dreams

Stepping through the veil
An emerald path ahead
Bare feet tread on velvet
Am I walking among the dead?

Moonlight filters through the treetops
Gossamer canopy overhead

Calm serenity around me

Yet me heart is filled with dread...

Summer

Legacy bound and
Memory burdened. Long days.
Shadows creeping in

Reminisce

8

The scent of earth laces the air
Golden light, warmest hue
Pine needles blanket the path ahead
Greenest grace fades into blue

Windswept vale, deepest breath
Water's edge meets shore imbued
Crest above, a rocky crown
Valley below, it's shadow consumes

Twilight devouring dusk
Moonlit heavens, stardust suffuse
Tranquility of the vespers
Reminisce my memories of you

Periwinkle

9

Hazy humid air
Warmest summer breeze

Turquoise sky above
Intertwining with the trees

Chicory laced meadows
Forget me nots in bloom

My not so distant memories
Reminding me of you

Raspberries

Roaming through thickets
Dense and overgrown
Hunting for memories
You and I had once known

Bright red and scarlet
Plucked straight off the vine
Sweetness turned bitter
A memento of time

Dream

Lightning flashes in the distance
Thunder rumbles in my bones
Rain comes crashing downwards
Wet clay squelching between my toes

As I try to walk forward
I sink deeper to my elbows
On the shore stands a figure
My hand extends towards

As I drag myself closer
The silhouette implodes
I look in my hand
And you left me a rose

Autumn

12

Crisp air and cool wind
The time for rest approaches
Crowning leaves descend

Campfire

Golden sparks leaping
Into brisk fresh air
The warmth of the embers
We gather to share

Surrounded by Timbers
Emerald guardians tall
Moon dust and glitter
As shooting stars fall

The seat you leave empty
A void unfulfilled
Your memory yet guiding
Your spirit here still

Hope Disheartened

14

Copper, gold and crimson
Blanketing the ground
Twig formed hands grasp skyward
Ethereal light surrounds

Bluest waters turn to black
Warm summer has adjourned
The melancholy howl
Of icy winds return

Dwindling

15

Heavy heart of burden
A legacy to leave
Fleeting moments so uncertain
Searching for reprieve

Steadfast marching onward
Resolution giving way
Progressively more tired
Perseverance slowly starts to decay

Dream of Death

Overcast and grey

Bleak bitter gusts of wind

Skeletal trees

Silhouetted against an October sky

Dead leaves trembling

Crumbling underfoot

I walk a cobblestone path

Strewn with brittle moss and weeds

The path curves sharply

Turning corners I cannot see

Fallow branches above me

Abruptly unveil a courtyard

In the centre a lone tree stands

Stark and bare it looms

Crimson stippled branches

Inching ever closer

Eyes adjusting to the gloom

Revealing, no rose of red,

Instead, I see before me

A tree of thorns and bramble

With crimson spots of blood

Adorned with corpses of hummingbirds

Crucified on thorns

Winter

18

Snowflakes' soft descent
Coating the world in silence
The earth laid to rest

Letting Go

A cloak of white surrounding
Softly cushioning all sound
The time of rest approaching
To leave behind your earthly bounds

Last Dance

Strong arms once guiding me
Weakened and brittle with pain

It's my turn to hold you
My cheeks with tears stained

As I carry you to the doorway
You stop me, voice strained

Taking my hand in yours
Saying, look, we are dancing again

Visit

Willow trees surrounding
Clover grasses coat the floor
Placing roses on your tombstone
I sit to talk with you once more

I brush away the debris
Clearing your name to read
I feel you here beside me
Your voice I long to heed

I give into despair
Sobbing in my grief
I draw a deep breath inward
Knowing in my heart you will be.

Dream of Moon Dust

A raven carries me

Soaring high above the tallest trees
Feathers glistening in the sun

A rush of wind carries us higher

We glide through the clouds
Shrouded in their soft embrace
Bursting through the cotton canopy

To come face to face
with the moon

The stars embrace us
Exploding into a shower of silvery moon dust
and golden sparks
Swirling faster and faster
A whirling stream of colour and light

Darkness.

I awake, eyes open, tears streaming down my
face.